VIRG[IN]

WITH A

VISION

SEX IS A GIFT; I'LL OPEN IT AFTER MARRIAGE.

POEMS BY
IKE EKWUEME

Virgin With A Vision
Copyright © 2020 Ike Ekwueme

Books may be purchased in quantity and/or special sales by contacting the publisher, Ike Ekwueme, by email at ekwueme.ike@gmail.com.

Editing and Formatting: Tanisha Stewart
www.tanishastewartauthor.com

Cover Design: Tyora Moody
www.tywebbincreations.com

First Edition

Published in the United Kingdom
by Ike Ekwueme

Contents

Introduction – why am I writing this book?

I have wrestled with thoughts about this book for years: *Who do you think you are writing a book like this? This is a sensitive topic; you will offend some people.*

Do you even have experience?

My answer is yes, I have experience at not having sex. I am very experienced at it.

What if, after writing this book – you end up having sex before marriage? What if people mock you for being a 28-year-old virgin? What if? What if?

In this day and age, it's not really 'cool' for a 28-year-old male to be writing about being a "virgin". As you can imagine, this is one of those books that could attract humiliating comments. I'm okay with that.

I had other books that I wanted to publish, but something within me said, "Write the book you are afraid to write."

To be honest, this is one of the deepest pieces of work I've written, because it is so personal. It is also about a sensitive topic which people don't often talk about openly and honestly. Hopefully, the contents of this book can be good conversation starters.

The truth is, I didn't write this book to brag or to make anyone feel guilty. Who am I to do that? I've been in many risky and heated situations but I didn't cross the line. How? I still don't know! It was not by my strength because I know what my body wanted to do in the moment but I just couldn't do it. Sex is a big deal!

If you've had sex before marriage, it doesn't make you "second-class" or "used" or any other degrading word you can think of. Although that lifestyle may have been your past, it doesn't have to be your present or future. You can choose to surrender your sexuality to God and trust Him for grace and strength to follow His ways. After all, He created sex.

I wrote this book to creatively share my journey, my story, and my struggles as a young Christian man in today's world. I wrote this book to inspire all my brothers and sisters out there to stand strong and hold onto their values. The peer pressure is strong, but we can choose to stand out. Sexual purity is possible.

There are many poems in this book that touch on a wide range of issues. I realize that sex is a big subject and I didn't cover all aspects. So if you see any gaps, I didn't chose to skip over those issues. I wrote as I was inspired to write. Maybe it will appear in the 2nd edition.

I used poetry to communicate in this book because I believe poetry has the power to simplify a message and amplify its impact on the reader. Also, poetry is a creative way to introduce such a sensitive topic and start an in-depth discussion.

In this book, you may see some words that you may consider "slang" or "graphic". I understand that these words may not be in your everyday vocabulary. This book is targeted at a broad audience. I used certain words to relate to my readers in different settings. Let us be honest with ourselves, as much as we may not want to admit it, even the children of today are using these words or hearing these words being used. Let your shock or disgust motivate you to pray for this generation.

As you read, if you have any questions, concerns, feedback or if you need more clarity on anything I wrote, feel free to contact me. Please note, the words in this book were written by me but they were inspired by various personal experiences and the experiences of others. I stood in other people's shoes as I wrote some of the poems. I hope that something in this book blesses you.

Dedication

First and foremost, I would like to thank God for sustaining me all these years and giving me the wisdom, insight, creativity and boldness to share this message. I am what I am by the grace of God. In my own strength, I am not qualified to share this message. If not for the grace of God, I would be living a life that is opposite to the values of this book.

I want to thank my parents for setting a Godly example for me in this area. My dad and mum married as virgins. My dad was in his thirties. Wow! It is not my desire to be single till thirty, but if he can do it – so can I, by God's grace.

My older brother has set a good example. My older sister has set a good example. According to birth order, I'm the third so it looks like I'm next. Hopefully I'll meet my wife soon. At the time I am writing this book, I haven't seen her yet. But the good news is, she is alive and well somewhere. Pray for me!

I would like to thank everyone who has inspired me to believe that it is possible to honor God's word and wait till marriage to have sex.

I also dedicate this book to everyone out there who is trying to do the right thing – the Godly thing. It is not easy to follow God's ways in the world we live in. There are a lot of noises, voices, choices, options, and temptations. I feel what you feel. Stay strong. With God, we will overcome.

"The only temptations that you have are the same temptations that all people have. But you can trust God. He will not let you be tempted more than you can bear. But when you are tempted, God will also give you a way to escape that temptation. Then you will be able to endure it." (1 Corinthians 10:13, ERV)

I pray that something in this book will inspire you to stay on the pure road and do the right thing - the Godly thing. It's not easy but with God - it's possible. God loves you and I love you too.

It is everywhere

In this generation
There's no shortage of inspiration
Everywhere you turn - provocation

It's even changing our communication
Simple words like spoon
Have a sexual connotation

We've drifted
Shifted
Our minds are afflicted
Polluted
We're spiritually diluted

Brains with twisted minds
We don't see faces anymore
All we see is her behind

What is all this?

Teenage pressure
Pursuit of pleasure
They say virginity is overrated
Give out your treasure

We see sex as leisure
It's a distorted view
Just because I like you
It doesn't mean that I have to have sex with you

Who is teaching all of you?
Who are these teachers?
Twisting God's word
And raising unbelievers

The truth they know

They begin to doubt
Can't speak up
So they close their mouth

Suffering in silence
Voice taken - can't shout
They want to go north
But the crowd is going south

Pressure to follow them
And do what they do
If we don't do what they do
They won't like me and you

Young kids seeing adult things
Doing adult things
Without true understanding
Of the consequence it brings

You probably sense my frustration
The concentration of sex
Is affecting our concentration
We can't even have a basic conversation.

He doesn't care about what's in her head
Or on her head
As long as she's breathing
He's willing to go ahead!

What is that all about?!

Love is work
But is there commitment today?
If you stop liking them – just leave
That's the teaching nowadays

Where is this leading us?

Single baby mama

Baby mama drama
Look around - no papa
Daddy just wants to hammer

We need to be concerned
We are building on a faulty foundation
Everything is sexualized
Is this helping our generation?

We have more "likes"
But are we truly happier?
We have more "friends"
But are we actually "friendlier"?

Not really...

Sex is like a wild animal
When you let it loose
You can't control what it does
You cannot choose

So, what we see today
Are the fruits
Of the wrong views of sex
Planted in the youth

We need to back up
Let's go back to God's original intention
He created sex
Before we start building - let's lay a strong foundation

Let us start honest conversations
Don't wait for a "situation"
Prevention is better than cure
The truth is real medication.

What is going on?

I asked her...
What is going on?

What do you mean?

I'm slightly confused...
Why is it so easy?
So easy to find...
So cheap...
You don't even have to look for it...
You don't even have to work for it...
No one is making anyone wait for it...
It's on sale everyday...
Casual... quick... on the way...
Just passing through...
A bit of fun...
No harm done...
In and out... got to go...

She said...
Hey, it's just an exchange...
Nothing more... nothing less...
No strings... just a fling... slide up my dress
He knows... I know...
No one is getting used...
Simple transaction... consensual...
What's there to lose?
Win - win...
Who's next?
Living my best life...

Is it the best though? Is this life?

Yes....

Really?

Is this what the Creator originally intended?

Well... Love is evolving - monogamy is dissolving
Get with the program... don't be so boring...

Do you think this is a problem worth solving?

She continued...
Sure... if you like...If you want to...
But I don't really see a problem... or maybe I'm in too deep to
see the way out...
Too numb to feel or care about what you're talking about
I'm making money with my mouth...
I don't even need to talk... just put it in and out.

Maybe the young will listen to the words coming out of your
mouth...
The young... but you're young
The younger young... the youth
Catch them before the media teaches them lies painted as
truth... or their friends...

I know how it ends...

What do you mean?

Me! I am how it ends.

I don't understand.

She explained...
I am how it ends
When you try to please fake friends
I am how it ends
When you try to fit in and blend
I am how it ends
When you don't listen to advice. They said go straight - I took a
bend
I am how it ends

When you try to get with a guy because he drives a Benz
I am how it ends
When you want to follow the trend...
I am how it ends
When you don't think about texts before you send.

You are not how it ends
You may be how it begins
But you don't have to continue because
Jesus died for your sin

Sexual sin?

Every kind
All of yours
And all of mine

I am just as sinful as you
You are not worse than me
In God's eyes
All sins weigh equally

As his children
He wants us completely free
The process starts with surrender
Would you like to pray with me?

(She's crying) Yes...

Please repeat after me...

"Lord Jesus...
I surrender my life to you
I have been living a lie
Help me to live the truth.

I am a sinner
Forgive me my sins
I've been losing in life

Help me to win

I thank you for this moment
I surrender to your ways
Not my will but your will
In Jesus' Name, I pray

Amen".

Virgin Loud, Virgin Proud

I'm a virgin, loud and proud;
Everyone may be having sex but I don't follow the crowd.

You are frigid, they say; you can even call me a freezer.

I'm keeping this for my wife; when I marry her –
 I will please her.

It's true I know, it's the 21st century

But that doesn't mean I have to have sex
With whoever is next to me.

Ike, Ike, Ike, you don't know what you're missing.
Am I really missing?

All this messing leads to stressing –
I'll pass on this casual sex thing.

The longer the wait, the sweeter it becomes

Don't worry; I will introduce my wife when she comes.

All this whining and grinding, it looks like sex to me

Yes they've got clothes on but I don't want her
Waking up next to me.

That's how it starts, I've seen it

It starts with a dance and then they both exit.

Take her home, you don't even know her name

It's a spiritual connection: this is not a game.

They say as men, we haven't got much to lose

We don't even need to wake up; we can just hit the snooze.

He brought her close and then he pushed her far

She's a human being bro; she's not a roller coaster.

He took her for a ride, and then he sent her outside.

It's so sad; all he wanted was her backside.

You bought her some booze then took her on a cruise

You were the only one; she didn't have anyone else to choose

And even though she's loose, that's no excuse.

She likes you, and she wants to stay overnight

I know you have your own house, but is it right?

It might be cool for you to tick her off your list

I respect God bro - I don't want to see His fist.

They say do it for today; don't worry about tomorrow

But if I do it today, I will wake up with sorrow.

The pressure is a lot; it's everywhere without measure

But I've held it for too long; I can't give away my treasure.

If you're after this gift, I'm sorry you will have to shift

I'm a man on a mission; I will not drift.

God is my strength; He is helping me every day

And by God's Grace you will hear my full testimony one day.

Yes, it's a high price to pay, but I prefer this way

You know what? I don't even want foreplay.

Don't worry; one day, I will have this sex thing

When you're married to her, you can have everything.

Yes, all the joy that it brings.

But there's a time for everything

Right now, as a single man, I don't want anything.

I've tried; I'm tired

My spirit wants to live for God
But my body wants to sin
My face is smiling
But I'm fighting a war within

Tall, short, thick and thin
My body wants them all
Not many things can trip me up
But I know women can make me fall

I like women
I'm a man - God designed me to
She has the door - I have the key
But you're telling me not to enter until I say "I do"

This purity thing is tough
I've tried but I'm getting tired
28 years - inspired
My organs are hot like fire
Seeking release
God please... I'm on my knees

You created sex
Then said marriage is the place to consummate
Left and right I'm hearing guys penetrate
But you're telling me to wait
I haven't even got a girlfriend -
So, when's my wedding date?

What's the point?
What's the point in waiting?
My body wants sex
What's the point in Christian dating?

God, I want to skip dating
And start procreating - I'm deliberating
Because this waiting

Is getting frustrating

Wait...Wait...Wait...

God I'm asking you
To get your permission
As I go to sin
Cover me on this mission

I am going to go in the sacred place
Once or twice
I know you will forgive me
Because you forgave them guys

After all their fornication
And all their lies
You still forgave them
God, you are really nice

So, I thank you in advance
For the pleasure I will enjoy
Don't be angry with me though
I know sin makes you annoyed

"Are you done?" says God.

Yes I created sex
Within marriage - it is holy fun
Outside marriage - like a fire it can burn
Many have scars
Do you want some son?

You've been running a tough race
Stay on the run
Don't let the enemy distract you
You've almost won

He's attacking more than ever
Do not accept defeat

Do not enter the sin pool
I know you're feeling heat

Don't let those evil thoughts
Trick you into a trap
You've come too far
To think of turning back

From the east to the west
From the north to the south
You've held on for this long
Please, don't tap out!

What are your goals?

It's amazing how well you can get to know a person when sex is not the destination of the "conversation".
What are your goals?

A happy life. A happy marriage. Happy relations.

Buildings that stand strong and long have a solid foundation. I've learned, to build a strong foundation for the marriage relationship, start by removing sex from the dating equation.

Focus on genuine communication: What do you have in common? What are your goals and visions? What do you like to watch on television?

From what I have seen, sexual interaction without a strong foundation leads to rapid depreciation – your value for the person decreases, your dislike of the person might even increase and you might have got yourself a bonus pack of sexually-transmitted diseases.

What are your goals?

They say this sex thing is the best thing; smash one, pick a next thing, body 1, body 2, keep counting. If she wants it, I'll give her the ding-a-ling.

Wait a minute darling, you're adding - you're counting!
Does that make you something? Come on; that's nothing.

As soon as you discover that she is not your type,
stop the hype.
If you are not interested in marrying her, don't use her for sex.

I know men are wired different; no attachment – who's next.

14

What are your goals?

If you say you love her and you want to marry her, and you actually care,
Let that love motivate you to quickly prepare. You don't need to put any mark on her body saying, "I woz ere".
Been there – done that. I had her first but you seconded that.
Bro, stop all that chat.

Prepare for what? Prepare for marriage. After that, she's yours till old age.
As I said before, intercourse before marriage can lead to carnage; because of one night, everything you built could be thrown in the garbage.

If you don't see her as a future wife that's okay.
Someone else will cherish her; let her go her own way.

You can call me old school; you can call me old fool,
You can call me frigid,
You can call me not cool,
You can call me bachelor; you can call me amateur,
I don't want to eat my future today – that's for sure.
And that's why I endure.

What are your goals?

I don't know about you, but I'm that kind of guy,
I want to hold myself to God's standards; I want to aim high,
I want a good wife; I want a good life,
I am doing this because I understand why,
The truth is though; I am tempted every day –
This is the truth - I'm not going to lie.

What are you building on?

The mouth may be saying
"I love you"
because that's what people say.

But you actually mean
"I lust you"
because you want them in bed one day.

It happens
It's natural
We're humans
We're sexual.

But we need to think
We are rational
Is this true love?
Or is it casual?

What are you building on?

The relationship will go bust
If you build it on lust
After a while
You will see the dirt and the dust.

Lust is a weak bond
That's why we didn't last long
When the winds of life became strong
We fell apart; our foundation was wrong.

Building on physical attraction
Is natural but not practical
The journey is too long
To be fuelled by only the sexual.

There's got to be other things
Or else someone may end up cheating,
When you build with wisdom and love;
Even when one person is absent for a while
That love will keep on heating.

Talk More, Touch Less

Before we start, I want to say that I believe in marriage.
I don't believe in picking up
and dropping relationships like luggage.
Also, I don't believe in treating women like garbage.

Personally, I eventually want to marry.
One day I want to be called daddy
But God taught me some things to do before I marry.

Talk more, touch less
Get to know her first or else your relationship will be a mess.
Don't rush the process.

If the only thing you are attracted to
are the features under her dress
I have to tell you bro - you are heading for stress.

She may have nice extensions; her backside gets your attention
But make a decision to have meaningful conversations
Or else, sooner or later, there will be tension.

Build your relationship on a spiritual foundation
You will enjoy it better when you delay gratification.

I know she's good to hold, especially when it's cold
There are many mysteries about her that you are yet to unfold
You probably wouldn't progress if you were told.

When she touches you, your head starts to swell
She also has a voice; have you heard her yell?
Find out brother, or else you are heading for hell in a cell.

When you touch her, you feel good
When you see her, you get in a happy mood

Because you didn't ask her, you didn't know she can't cook
Food is not everything
But it's important that this part is understood.

She has big breasts, but every night you can't rest
Is this the kind of relationship you want? Do you honestly
want to be depressed?
Take your eyes off her chest.
Talk to her and find out what she likes best.

I know you like her when it's sunny
I hope you still have love for her when life is not funny.
She will be your wife for life;
she must forever be your only honey
That's why you have to make sure before starting the journey.

If you didn't know this part, you better not start
I hope you know now, it is till death does you apart.

That's why I said; focus on the spiritual not the physical
I know it's hard; we're human beings, it's natural
Get to know her: put aside the sexual.
Rub minds together – that's intellectual
I can only advise you, but it's your choice; you're an individual
But I've tried this approach - it's so beneficial
Many people say they like to touch - it's not accidental
Whatever you sow you will reap - it's scriptural.

Some say I need to sleep with her to really know
if she is the one
I need the practice and I need the fun
This is bad advice; you may end up with a son
You can't handle this responsibility, and you may run.

There are many great women potentially

But you need to approach relationships gradually
Focus on building each other up spiritually
It may be hard at first, but you will get there eventually
Life will be so sweet; you will live together happily.

Don't start the engine

"I didn't plan to go all the way"
That's a common regret people say today
But the journey to sex began
When you started hanging out with foreplay.

When you start the engine
It might be difficult to stop
It's also difficult to press the brakes
When you're already on top

He's already at top speed
Now you're telling him to wait
At this point
It might be too late

If you don't want to get burnt
Don't play with fire
If you don't want to get electrocuted
Don't go near the wire

Don't push the boundaries
Stay away from the line
Don't even let the thought
Stay in your mind

How far is too far?
How far can I go?
If I were you
I wouldn't even start the journey bro

I know you say
"We are just friends"
But remember what I said
About how this journey ends.

Set straight boundaries
Don't allow bends

And avoid those sexy messages
That you normally send

Don't awaken sex
Until the time is ripe
Because when water starts flowing
It's difficult to stop the pipe.

We should have waited

They said...

We thought nothing would happen
But it did and then we hid
Like Adam and Eve in the garden
Embarrassed, shame, guilt, naked

The fire was starting
We saw it coming
But we enjoyed the warmth
Until it starting burning

By the time we realized
It was too late to run
We both reached the point
Of no return

We couldn't stop the motion
We had to ride out the storm
No protection
Will a baby be born?

You may think you are standing tall
But you can still fall
Pride leads to destruction
I'm quoting bible verses that's all

If I like you
And you like me
Chilling in your room
Is very risky
I know people say "we will not have sex"
But after kissing and touching - what is next?

We could've, We should've
But we didn't wait
This would have been sweeter

On the wedding date

Our boundaries were weak
We were dancing on thin ice
We both lost our virginity
8pm that night

We should have waited
Argh! Can we rewind time?
I shouldn't have gone to her house
At that time!

If you dance close to the line
You are likely to cross
I thought I was strong
I thought I was a boss

I thought it could only happen to them
Definitely not me
Now we've had sex
I feel guilty

Guilt, shame
I've been preaching Jesus' name
Will our relationship
Ever be the same?

We both feel like
We let ourselves down
The royal wedding was set
But now we have no crown

God please forgive us
We feel really bad
God has forgiven us
But we still feel sad

Listen world
Sexual purity is not outdated

Waiting till marriage is possible
We should have waited.

I felt like a thief

A guy said to me....

Every time I slept with her
I felt like a thief
It was like I stole the room, the woman,
And the bedsheets

I was using something I didn't buy
It also wasn't given to me
I took advantage
Of a vulnerable opportunity

It was sweet when it was happening
We made love to songs
But I would go home thinking
This is so wrong!

Every time I slept with her
I felt like a robber
Because I would eat at her house
But she wasn't my last supper

It took me a while to realize
Where the guilt came from
And it wasn't because
I didn't use a condom

It was because....

Sex is marriage
Having sex is saying "I marry you"
We were not married
So I was just using you

Yes, it was casual but consensual
We are both intellectual
She thought I was committed

But I was off to my next schedule

I am not married to her
This is not my wife
I was just trying to get a quick high
Then get on with life

I was married with my body
But my mouth never said "I do"
Anytime she would talk of marriage
I would make an excuse

I convinced myself to believe that
I have nothing to lose
I felt like a thief every time
I was the chief of abuse

That life is wrong
I've changed my ways
God had mercy
I'm a living testimony today

I'm sharing my story
With the next generation today
Sex is a lifelong film
But after marriage is when you press play.

Beat it, Bang it, Smash it

You say you want to:
Beat it
Bang it
Smash it
Destroy it
Tap it
Bash it
Pound it
Break it
Chook it
Dagger and Penetrate...
That's how people get STDs mate.

Beat it, bang it, and smash it and dash
When it's time to go home, you give her the cash

You want to dagger it, bang it and destroy,
Let us stop using women like toys.

You're treating women like that
Imagine if someone did that to your sister?
How would you feel if someone
Used her, abused her, kissed her and dissed her?

See - you wouldn't like it; you're getting angry already
What if it was your mother?
Okay then, so stop treating women like steps
Skipping from one to another.

You want to smash, bash, and dash,
You're talking about women like trash.
To another man,
You may look powerful
But to a woman,

This is very disrespectful.

Riding Chicks like bikes

He said: "I've been riding chicks like bikes"
Bro, do you want a medal?
I've been asked to hop on couple times
But I didn't step on the pedal

Please don't come here
Trying to make me feel insecure
I think you need self-control
You might be a bit immature.

You're trying to make me feel like a disgrace
You're trying to make me feel like I'm losing the race
The difference between me and you is that
I had the discipline to say no to their face.

I've had opportunities
Here and there
I'm not saying I'm a babe magnet
But I've had my fair share

I said no
When she offered to blow
Sorry, I've got standards
This is too low.

You want to be known as that guy
Who rides chicks like bikes
Well, I want to be known as that guy
Who God likes.

We all need to be careful
Because our actions are seeds we sow
What you plant today
You will eat tomorrow

The seeds we plant
One day, we will see the fruit

I want to set an example
For my children and other youth.

Let me also add...

These "chicks" may not have a dad
But they have a God
Have you checked?
Look what He said in His Word

You're playing tricks
Marking ticks
Check out the consequences
1 Thessalonians 4 verse 6

I don't want to be punished
Do you?
That scares me bro
It should scare you

I want to be known for
Self-control, integrity and dignity
You might not rate me
But God rates my virginity.

A sister for a sister

Do you have a sister?
Yes.
How old is she?
24
Oh great, same age as this girl too.

I had a thought
Since the girl you are with is someone's sister
And since you have a sister
Let's sign a gentleman's deal.

Whatever you do to her
Some guy will do it to your sister too.
If you treat her like crap
Your sister will be treated like poo.

The day you ask her to clean
Your sister will be on her knees
The day you ask her to cook
Your sister will be making rice and peas

There are some acts
That are very shallow
If you ask her to open her mouth
Your sister must swallow

Such a great idea isn't it?
I've added a twist to the game
If you want to be a 'playa'
Your sister will be played the same

It's really interesting
When you think of it like this
If you ever wee on his sister
Your sister will be sprayed with piss

Whatever level of contact you decide

Will be reciprocated
If you force her to sleep with you
Your sister will be penetrated

If you treat her with respect
Your sister will be treated with dignity
If you take advantage of her
Your sister will lose her virginity

Whatever you do to her
To your sister - it will get done
If you make her look stupid
Your sister will put a bag on

Sorry to be too graphic
What happens today is tragic
Just to have sex with one girl
Many guys are queuing like traffic

I repeat, this is the contract
Whatever you do
Your sister will get it back
If you give her a whack
Your sister will get a smack!

If you take from her like a thief
Your sister will experience grief
If you suddenly decide to leave
Your sister will be dumped by Steve

If you choose to do what is right
And wait until you marry
Your sister will find Mr. Right
His name might even be Harry.

It's really simple
It's not complicated
Be a nice guy
Don't let her be manipulated

Listen, even if she's no one's sister
She is God's creation
She is not an object
For your personal stimulation

I've signed my part
Now it's over to you
Please sign on the dotted line
If the contract is okay with you

Now that it's signed
We both know what to do
Do unto others
As you would like them to do to you.

The pressure is on

If you think this one could be for life
Why let a few minutes spoil it?
After marriage she is yours
It's worth the wait - you will enjoy it.

Yes, a few minutes - let's say five
We all have the drive
But you don't have to dive
Especially if you believe this one is for life.

Cherish her, nurture her, care for her - don't puncture her
The focus is conversation not penetration,
Getting to know each other on a deeper level
This is real education.

The easiest thing to do is sex.
She wants it. He wants it. They do it.
But to me, there is power in not doing it
And waiting till the wedding day.
Am I the only one that thinks this way?

Some may say I'm talking too much;
Sex is not a big deal
If I want it, I do it, whenever I feel.
Okay, that's you but let me share my truth:
I don't think that approach to sex is sustainable
It is not a standard we can set for the youth.

Eventually, someone will get hurt
Someone will get used
Someone could get raped
Someone could get abused

Whenever sex is brought in, things change

Things can get a little awkward and a little bit strange.
I've seen them naked,
Right - what else is there to know?
Nothing much, so one person decides to go
The famous lines are released, "It's not you - it's me –
I think I better leave"
It's over; the whole thing ends in grief.
They say that's life; it wasn't meant to be
I get that part but she still has a piece of me.

Move on. It's not easy; how can I?
This guy has seen my front and backside.
If I didn't give him my body
I wouldn't be in so much pain.
I've learned my lesson
I'm not doing that again.

But the same thing can happen in marriage
True! But the commitment to marry
reduces the potential damage
It's not a case of, tonight I'm in and tomorrow I'm out
You'll remember the wedding vows
you made with your mouth.

The people that pressure you to give out your treasure
Don't understand that the consequences are beyond measure.

In high school
If you haven't kissed a girl, you were not cool
If you haven't had sex, you were old school.
The hype started when I was about twelve
Pressure from right and left
But I thank God that I didn't sell myself.

I went to university when I was eighteen;
I had self-confidence and a good self-esteem.

I admit it was difficult,
I think I was the odd one out on the team.
The only one who hasn't seen
The only one who hasn't been
The only one who hasn't had sex on the soccer team.

This is my testimony.
I'm not out to condemn anybody;
I'm that kid that's waiting for the marriage ceremony.
I pray God holds us in holy matrimony
Every day, we will be singing songs of harmony.

Dad, there's this girl

Dad, there's this beautiful girl
I love her reflection
She's gorgeous
But she's becoming a distraction.

She walks by
She gets my attention
She touches me
Sudden erection.

Every conversation
It's her that I mention
Once, I put myself in trouble
To see her in detention.

She feels the same way
It's a mutual emotion
I don't even read my Bible anymore
She is my devotion.

Son, I can see she's an attraction
But a girl that stops you from reading your Bible
Is more than a distraction
I think you need to take immediate action.

No closed-door interactions
This could lead to intercourse action
Avoid late night discussions
This can lead to temptation
I know what I'm saying
Only open space communication.

Son, I love you and I know your frustration
I know how you feel

But wait till after graduation
If you think she's the one - marry her
I'll pay for the wedding, reception and vacation.

You will have my support
But for now, I need you to follow my instruction
Focus on your books
Make an impact on your generation
Son, trust me, even if she's not the one
There are many women in every nation.

The daddy influence

One of the big things for me was...

My earthly father modelled my heavenly father (God)
I grew up with this consistent picture
If my dad was a wild dude
I probably would have twisted some scriptures

I have been in some places and spaces
Where l wanted to commit sexual sin
But I remembered what daddy said
I stopped when I remembered him

If he would have crossed the line
I would have thought it was fine
You've made your mistakes dad
Allow me to make mine

But he didn't.
He didn't fall for this temptation
So he set the foundation
For the next generation

A lot of inspiration
Has come from observation
University was a big test
But I made it to graduation

I tell you the truth
No word of a lie
If my dad was a "playa"
I would have probably tried

And I wouldn't feel bad about it at all
Adam fell, Dad fell - every man will fall

Save sex till marriage
I understand why

My dad did it
Extra motivation to try

I do understand - it's my life
And I can live it
But I've learned some disciplines
To my children - I will give it

He's not perfect
Nowhere near
But the fear of God is in Him
You can see the fear

When the father figure in your life
Is following the Bible
Even though he could go the other way
It inspires you, it drives you
It makes you endure just one more day

Thank God – honestly, I thank God for him
If not for my earthly example
I would have freely entered acts of sin

He still cares about the little things too
Here and there
At my age
He is still concerned about my hair

Don't do that hair style
It makes you look mad
Everywhere you go as a son
You represent Dad

Like Father like son
You know the saying
My father wasn't a playa
So I'm not playing

He stayed with one wife

So I am staying
In God I trust
Day out and day in

This is my story
I'm just saying what I see
Dad controlled himself
So we thought... okay, so can we

I'm grateful for my earthly father
And the good examples around me
Thanks for being a good influence
In this area of sexuality.

I know their address

If I wanted to talk to dirty
I know who to call
If I wanted temptation
I know where to fall

Friends with benefits
I know who to text
No strings attached
Have fun and sex

If I wanted it
They're on my phone
Some are in London
I know their zone

I'm not saying
I get girls like that
I'm just saying
I know where the sex is at

It's located near me
Probably near you too
Some go there often
But that's not my advice to you

Just because you can
Doesn't mean you should
Yes it's true
There are people out there who would have sex with you

Paid or unpaid
Even if it's free
You have to put more worth
On your body

Stop giving yourself like that
Casually...

Honestly...
Sex is more than two bodies

It's the truth
I can keep going and going
I was in the dark before light came
Now I'm glowing and growing

The body wants to
But the spirit said "don't participate"
Casual sex is sweet
But it leaves a bitter aftertaste

You will enjoy this sex food
After your wedding date
You can eat all that's on the plate
Start early and finish late

No guilt or shame
God says go ahead
This is your house, your wife
and this is your bed

To me, this is the best type of benefits
Because my wife is my friend
Which means our love story
Doesn't have to end.

She's dangerous

Hey guys,
Something you need to know
There are some girls in this world
That can't tell a guy no.
After you
She gets on your bro.
She stays the night
In the morning, she says, "Got to go".
She is messing up many people's lives
But she doesn't care, so...
Whatever she offers you
Just tell her no.
Even if she asks for a job and says
"I just want to blow".
I know it's hard
But still tell her no.
You will lose your reputation
Is it worth it? No!
Stay away from these women
I'm telling you now so you don't say, "I didn't know".

Her dress
Gets the guys attention.
They are hypnotized
Until they enter detention.
She knows she's attractive
She's an attraction.
When she walks in
She's a distraction.
She knows what she's doing
She's a temptation.
Tempting guys to get their participation
Stay away guys, she's looking for action
She's dangerous;

She'll divide you like a fraction.

How did it all happen?
You can't even mention
Let me tell you,
It all started when you gave her attention.

Men are moved by what they see

Dear ladies, my dear sisters all over the world...

I just wanted to let you know,
Men are moved by what they see.
When you decide to put your body on show
I will explain what happens in our minds
In case you didn't know.

What you show can take our mind to places that we were not planning to go.
And our bodies may even follow.
Sexual thoughts coming fast and slow
Sexual positions; high and low
This is what is happening in our minds when you decide to wear those clothes
And I think some of you already know.

"But he's not a robot," she said... "I didn't make him do anything though,"
I know,
You may not be responsible for his actions: the filthy communication, molestation, the exploitation - yes he took advantage of the situation. It was his decision.
But I just wanted to inform you that as a woman, your appearance can lead men into temptation.
You were beautifully endowed at creation but your appearance on occasions can be a distraction which can lead men to actions that will cause their condemnation.

I am not blaming you; I'm just making you aware of this situation.

You have power.
You have power.

As a woman whoever you are
You have power.
But, don't be part of the problem
Be part of the solution.

An individual's journey to salvation
May be caused by many people's contributions.
In the same way, an individual's journey to destruction
May have been stimulated by the actions of people in different
locations.

I'm not pointing a finger of accusation
I'm not telling you what to wear on vacation
I'm not giving you any description
I'm just giving a suggestion.
This information is for women and men in every generation.
Please, let your appearance not lead people into temptation;
rather, let it give God glory and adoration.

Your body is not for sale

Young lady – you are hot
I know your body can sell
But some of these pictures and videos
Are sending some men straight to hell

My dear sisters
We all know that sex sells
But you don't have to be the seller
Lies also sell
But you don't have to be the teller
It's true; you're an influencer
Please use this influence to make people's lives better

My aim is to encourage
Not to make you feel guilty
You may think it's just a picture
But the average man's mind is filthy

Images are seeds
Planted in the mind
All day he is thinking about your backside
And leaving his wife behind

He meditates
The thought marinates
He masturbates – ejaculates
After; he doesn't feel great

I know there is demand
But you don't have to supply
Your body is not for sale
Let them go elsewhere to buy

You have worth

You have value
You have virtue
Money can't buy you.

Great looks come with great responsibility

To all the babe magnets out there...

Bragging about how many you've had
Doesn't make you bad
It's actually kind of sad.
We need self-control
Not being able to control IT when IT goes hard
Is the same kind of spirit that makes people
Overspend on their credit card.

I know you're handsome and you look good
You say you get girls easily – understood.
But just because you can
Doesn't mean you should.

They like you
They want it
Okay, she is 'easy' to get
But you don't have to take it.
You said you're a real man bro
Real men don't say yes all the time
A real man would say no.

He said to me, "Hear me out,
It was just a quick one
Easy in, easy out
Bro, I didn't ask her anything
She volunteered and opened her mouth

It's not my fault
I can't let that opportunity go
If she's eager to do the job
It's rude to tell her no
So I let her blow".

Please listen bro
If something like this happens again
Tell her no
After that, tell her about her true worth
So she knows.

Bro, this girl is lost
She's been living a lie
Wasting her life
On different kinds of guys.
Even if she's loose
You don't have to make it wider
The average guy doesn't care
He just wants to get inside her.

The world is full of broken souls
Let us help them out
Don't dig a deeper hole
Let us save them - this should be our goal.

Especially you
And you know why
You used to be just like her
Living a lie.
Help her out
Point her to the Most high
Tell her about Jesus
He's the nicest guy.

Tell her, He came for you and me
I used to be the male version of you
But Jesus set me free.

My life was a mess
But the moment I believed

He took all the weights off me
Now I'm so relieved.

I confessed my sins
He took my anxieties and stress
He changed my name and my clothes
I am no longer a mess.

I'm no longer that guy
That everyone used to know
I'm a new creation
Clean, pure and white as snow.

My confidence is back
No more hiding in a cave
I'm as bold as a lion
My new name is Brave Dave.

Can I have your attention please?

I wore it
So they would see
I exposed some skin
So they would notice me.

That dress
Has caught many eyes
I'm tired of men
Just walking by.

You've got a nice shape
But you don't need to show every corner and curve
Save this eye candy
For the man who will deserve it.

I know they say if you've got it then flaunt it
Let them know it; show it
Post a pic – they will like it
Be hot and enticing.

Your heart is the cake
Your body is the icing
You've been exposed for a while
What have you been attracting?

Professional actors
Professional deceivers
Professional users
Professional leavers.

Hey lady,
I've got a man's mind
You're nice
But you're not the only one with a nice behind.

It's easy for a man to like your body
And love your chest
But there are many out there
What makes you stand out from the rest?

What will stop him from cheating?
What will make him pass the test?
When he sees another chest,
Trust me; he's not thinking about your breasts.
It's the value you bring
The stuff inside
I know you think you're nice
But have you seen her backside?

One guy said:
I eat well at home
So I don't eat junk outside
My wife is my friend
I don't want your backside.
Why? She asked.
You've got a nice backside
But my wife has a nice front side
We have a deep connection inside
Nothing can compare outside.

What I see in front
Makes up for the back
I see great things in our future
I don't want to look back.

Good communication is attractive
Become a friend
It's these intangible things
That has kept many couples going till the end.

Do you want attention?
Learn how to hold a conversation
I know they say let your body talk
But there's a lot of competition.

There are many bodies out there
Everywhere on display
I can tell you what might impress a godly man;
A woman that prays.

Nice container and she has content
This woman is a present.
Not just good for red carpet pictures
This woman is one for the future.

Don't worry about looking hourglass
Become first class
Valuable is attracted to value
The trash guys will pass.

What's inside?

Lads, are you looking for a woman?
Don't focus on the backside - focus on what is inside.
Yeah, "baby got back", but living with her might be crap.

Her appearance may seem nice,
Marriage is not for one week - this is for life.
You better wake up and open your eyes.
Marriage is not a gamble; don't roll a dice.

Pretty looking lady
Yes, no, or maybe?
The bigger question is
Do you want her to be the mother of your babies?

Nice looking container
But does she have content?
Does she really love you?
Or does she just want a percent?

You know how divorces work
Sometimes - everything splits in two
Don't wait till you're married
To discover who you're married to.

Fun then run

I don't recommend that kind of fun.
You may end up with a son.
He grows up with no man in his life
because his daddy has done a run.
Then society teaches him to protect himself by carrying a gun.
All this started because of 5 minutes of reckless "fun".

Beware ladies; they will call you "hun" until the fun is done.
When they find out you're pregnant - they're gone.
"It's not my son".
Don't be that guy. He calls her "hun" until the fun is done.
When the sun comes up or the son comes up – he's gone.

He's another guy who wants fun then runs
when the son comes.
You are worth more than that; don't leave your body
to be trampled on
Don't let guys use you to complete their home-run.
It's a hit and run strategy – they are looking for girls to use
You don't have to be the one.

If you don't want the son, then stay away from that type of fun.
Many people may persuade you,
but tell them you don't want none.
"I'm studying at the moment;
I'll marry and have that when I'm done".
My sperm is precious; I can't just waste it on anyone.
They are all doing it, but I'm an individual; I'm not everyone.
I'm not short-sighted; I'm thinking about the long-run.

The mama, the baby, the drama

He said, there's this girl...

I liked her
But I told her
I loved her
I slept with her
I stopped "loving" her
But she still loves me
But I don't love her
Why?
I never did
Remember my first statement
I liked her
Not even like, like - like
I just liked her body.

The drama continues...

She's pregnant
Who's the daddy? Me.
So I have a kid with her
But I don't like her
If I don't like her
Will I like the kid?
If I see the kid
I will see her face in the kid
And if I want to see the kid
I have to see her first
Because she is the mama
But I don't want to see her
Because I don't like her.
Am I really going through all this because of 7 minutes?

Where's my dad?

There was a child who didn't know his dad.
When he remembers, he feels sad.
"What did I do?" the child says.
"Did I do anything bad?"
"Where's my dad? Where's my dad?"
The kid grew up wishing he had
Someone he could look up to and call dad.

Don't Run Man

First it was just fun
In and out. I'm done. Gone.
Hold up bro. She's pregnant with your son.

Even though you're done with his mum
Take responsibility for your son
Don't Run.

Your child needs you
He needs both of you
I know this is not a situation that can be fixed with glue.
True - but what do we do?
What's done has been done. The son has come.
Now, what are you going to do?

I'm not saying make her your wife
I'm just saying be in his life.
Don't let the streets raise him
Because they'll teach him about the knife.

Life happens. Things happen.
I can't say that I know how you feel
I only pray that this injury will heal.

I pray that God shows you
What to do and where to go
It's easier to run – but don't
Stay there for your son bro.

For your son. For your son.
Do it for your son.
Don't run man - be there for your son.

Like Father, Like Son

The apple doesn't fall far from the tree
I'm not surprised by his behaviour
His dad said
He's a reflection of me

The fruit will naturally reflect
The seed that was sown
Unless the child decides to
Change on his own

At the time I thought
It's fun - just enjoy
I didn't know my actions
Would reproduce in my little boy

This thing called sex
Has a generational effect
I preach to him all day
Everything he rejects

Hold up, Dad
But you didn't wait
You weren't home on time
You came late

I'm lost for words
What can I say?
He's right though
But that's my yesterday

This girl and that girl
In the room; in the car
The injury has healed
But I still see the scar

Well... this is what I get
What did I expect?

This is one of my regrets
I tell people now - wait till marriage
Sex... don't open it yet

The good news is: today's a new day
Jesus has wiped all my sins away
But the consequences are still there
I still have to pay.

Yes, He paid the price
No more darkness - now I'm light
But my boy is still my responsibility
That can't change overnight

I'm still his dad
He's still my son
Because God sent His Son
Doesn't mean I'm free to run

This is not the dream picture
The feeling is very bitter
But I'll keep praying and believing
That things will get better.

Sex was my problem

He told me man to man:
Sex was the root of all my problems.

Because of sex I fumbled
Because of sex I rumbled
I used to be great
Because of sex I tumbled.

I had a good woman
We were a good couple
I was selfish;
I wanted double.

Like a lion in the jungle
I would hunt and hustle
This thing called sex
Has put me into a lot of trouble.

I was confident
I was a man with muscle
I thought sex was life
I was forcefully humbled.

I had fame
Girls shouting my name
I was playing the body count game
But no one told me that losing came with shame, pain
And my reputation would go down the drain.

Sex is a fire
Under control; it will warm up the house
Out of control; it destroyed my houses.
Under control; make love with only your spouse
Out of control; I drove away my spouses.

I dressed well
Nice shirt and trousers
The problem was
I struggled to zip up my trousers.

3 children
3 different mothers
Looking back now
Why did I bother?

I didn't actually get caught
I cheated and confessed
My life was simple
But reckless sex introduced stress.

I'm eating bitter fruits today
Because I planted the seeds
I'm telling you what I've done
But please don't follow my lead!

Sex is a gift; open it after marriage

Sex is a gift; I'll open it after marriage.
If I open it now, I know I will feel like garbage.
I'll wait till me and my wife are in holy unity
Then I can lose my virginity without feeling guilty.

Holy matrimony is the way to harmony;
When children come, it's a testimony.
But having sex early can cost you dearly
You'll be paying weekly, monthly and even yearly.

All you built has gone down the drain: graduation, reputation,
Just because of short term gain. Wow, what a shame!

Ike, look at Jane. Come on man; are you insane?
No, I train to abstain;
women like Jane are the source of all your pain.

What about Emily - she can't be boring in bed.
Please, don't lose your head; save your money instead
One step in her house – you're dead!

That's what happened to Dave,
now he's six feet under in the grave.
Just behave! Do you really want to spend eternity as a slave?

That's how sex is; it can happen quick and fast.
The pleasures are temporary;
then it leaves you regretting the past.
The "benefits" don't last.
Ask the guy who went out last night on a blast.

Before he was brave; but after that rave,
You won't find him out; he is hiding in a cave.
Crowd pleaser, woman teaser

Now he has no name; he's called that geezer.

Just because you got paid,
it doesn't mean you have to go out and get laid.
This lifestyle has caused many people's progress to be delayed
and their lives decayed.

Some people see sex as a game; be careful all "playas".
Sex may give you an appetizer of fame;
but the main course is shame.
Don't play that game. You will never be the same.

I prefer to live this way; yes it's a high price to pay
But it will be worth it in the end; I'll tell the world one day.
I'm looking forward to the day,
when I walk out with my wife and say
"Hey - it was worth the wait; with God - there's no delay!"
God's way is really the best way.

He's a Virgin

He's a Virgin - he's a Virgin
What is this that I am hearing?
He's a Virgin - he's a Virgin
Is it possible in this generation?

He's a Virgin
He hasn't slept around
He's a Virgin
He has no body count
He's a Virgin
He is not a clown
He's a Virgin
After marriage – he said he'll get down.

The bed is cold

My brothers, I understand
The bed is cold,
You need a woman to hold.
But getting a woman from the street, club, or wherever
is not the solution though.

Women come and go
What you need is a wife.
When you marry right,
The bed stays warm
Every single night.

Lonely times

Lonely evenings
Lonely weekends
Everyone's out
And you want to blend.
Everyone's going
And you want to attend.
But the Spirit is saying
Don't follow the trend.
I want you to have fun
But there's a kind of fun I don't recommend.

It's a war within
Do I follow God straight?
Or take a bend?
Stay strong my friend
This purity journey
Is worth it in the end.

I like you; you like me

If there's an attraction
Beware of distraction
You say you are just friends
But it's getting a bit intense
Establish boundaries;
Put the Bible as a fence

If me or you cross the line
This "friendship" has to end
Deal?
It's obvious that we like each other
Let's not pretend

I like you; you like me
But let us establish clear boundaries
So we don't get a little bit carried away
and end up in the same bed one day

I like you; you like me
Praying privately together is also a little bit risky
Because prayer has the power to make two people connect
Before you know it; it could lead to sex

I like you more than a friend
But I don't want our friendship to end
So let's find someone we are accountable to
So we don't divert from the purity road to a dead end

I like you; you like me
We're Christians but we are still human beings
Of course, we can still go out on dates
But we must honor God
Let's not bring shame to our faith.

I'm human like you

I've not had sex.
Many young people have
And they are telling me to go next.
I've had opportunities and I could do it but to be honest
I'd rather have God's best.

I used to do that whining and grinding
It was a long time ago.
But I stopped it
Because it was like having sex with clothes.

I know she knows how to twerk
But I don't want this kind of work.
How can I do this on Saturday night?
Then on Sunday dress up and go to church?

People ask me, how do I do it? It's not me.
It is God, He helps me
I am human, just like you.
I like women, I wouldn't mind two.

I've had opportunities
To have fun.
But when I see it coming
Something just says run.

God said stop
I said okay.
No questions,
I just obey.

If I continued that way
My life would have ended up in destruction
I'm so happy that I followed His instructions.

The Bible says,
Run from youthful lusts.
God has great advice
He wants the best for us.

Sex now, can make life complex
If you go under the dress
Be ready for whatever comes next.

One baby or two
Who's the father? Not me.
You knew you got her pregnant
But you denied it, "It wasn't me".

One woman or three
At the time it felt good.
Now they all call you daddy
You have to bring home the food.

I'm not ready for that
I don't want that life.
I only want one woman
I only want one wife.

It's strange I know;
People say you're young – have fun.
But I know how it all ends
That's why I run.

I want to enjoy life
But not that kind.
I only want one wife
One day – I will find.

The purity road

May not be for everybody.
But I've been told
I'm not just anybody.

My body is God's
He paid a high price.
Whenever you feel tempted, they say
Don't look - close your eyes.

I'm human like you
I'm tempted every day.
But I have a reward in heaven
That's why I live this way.

I'm happy; honestly I'm okay
It's worth the wait; I will have it one day.
When I get married
Play, Play, Play!

All this pleasure,
I'll get it one day.
Me and my wife
No rules; we will play, play, play!

Don't look at me like that.
She is mine.
Do you know how long I waited?
I waited a long time.

What's the problem?
She's my queen and I'm her king.
If you don't believe me
Look at the ring.

I will express myself
I am free.

I belong to her
She belongs to me.

Right now I'm single
But the temptation is on.
Many women walk past me
But I can only have one.

When I am ready and steady
I will go.
I desire a strong woman
Together, we will grow.

I'm almost there
I've gone too far to stop.
It doesn't matter what people think - I won't flop.
I'm aiming for the top and by God's Grace - I won't drop.

I feel what you feel

The same things you feel
I feel
I'm human like you
I chill
With the ladies
I have some skill
But when the sex thoughts come
I kill it!

It's not about how I feel
Listen, I signed a deal
No sex till marriage; it's sealed
No one can come and steal.

I don't know who you are
Together, let's raise the bar
I know living this way can be hard
But I can't go back,
Because I've come too far.

I see what you see, but I stop myself from clicking, clicking
I feel what you feel, but I stop myself from tickling, tickling
I smell what you smell, but I stop myself from licking, licking
I'm waiting for marriage, waiting for the wedding, the
wedding.
I'm human just like you, in case you were thinking, thinking.

Come to my house

She was in my class - teacher spoke, she didn't hear it...
The assignment was hard - she didn't get it...
She said to me "Stop by my house..."
I said, "I'll come and share it..."

Got to the house... Didn't expect it... she was waiting;
She was naked...
She was ready and steady... she wanted me to go...
My life flashed before my eyes and I said, *forget it*
If I do it tonight... tomorrow - I'll regret it.

She asked... "Should I put it on you?
Or do you wanna put it on me?"
Cus right now I'm feeling kinda horny,
I'm feeling sweet and sexy - I'm like honey in tea
I know you want a sip of me.

The tea looks good
But I'm okay,
I should probably be on my way
I'm not in the mood.
I already had some green tea back at the hood.

I'm a tasty sauce
Come and take a dip
I'm good thanks; I'll skip
I already had dinner before I came on this trip.

Are you sure you're not hungry?
I have something for your mouth
This is not my scene
I think it's time for me to go out.

(He walks out. She starts coming toward him)

I'm not hungry
I just came to give you a quick summary
Maybe we can meet tomorrow at break
At the library.

(He shuts the door and runs)

Why are you rushing?

If she's yours – you can wait. If he's yours – you can wait.
Go out on dates – become good mates
Do whatever you want – go on holiday to the States.

But don't rush to the bed.
It's not the most important thing
You shouldn't even be thinking about that
Her finger has no ring.

Engage your minds intellectually
Listen to the Spirit - do things spiritually.
If you want this relationship to stand strong and long
You can't lay the foundation bodily and casually.

They say you need to test-drive
No you don't, even if she's your wife to be.
If you believe she's yours
Then, you can wait patiently.

They say sex is a fun game; men and women play it too
I am more concerned about those coming behind you.
The next generation – seeing all this - hearing all that
If they haven't done it
People call them pussy cat.

They say do it, do it, do it, now
Do it, do it, do it anyhow
Do it, do it, do it today
But they won't be there to take care of your baby.

Some say sex is not a big deal
Show them how much you love them
Show them how you feel.

You see, they tell you to go in
But when they come out – they don't give you the review.
It's a one-sided advice –
there are some things they are not telling you.
How conversation has reduced, interaction has dropped
Meeting up – he makes an excuse
The relationship is about to stop.

She served him her body
He didn't work hard to eat
He's bored now
He's looking for fresh meat.
Your relationship is only as pure as the two people involved.
If both of you are committed to wait – problem solved.
But if one person is saying yes and the other is saying no
You have to decide – do I stay in these conditions or do I go?

Sow good seeds while dating; reap good fruits in marriage.
Sow bad seeds while dating; reap bad fruits in marriage.

I could but I won't

Just because you can,
Doesn't mean you should
Just because you could
Doesn't mean it's good.
She gave Joseph her body
He said, "I'm not in the mood".
How many guys would do that?
Many would eat it up like food.

I can't let him go

We break up today
Then we meet up the next
I feel attached to this guy
I can't sleep until I text

Quick question:
Have you had sex?
Yes.
And he was my best.

Okay. Continue...

When he doesn't reply
I feel like I want to cry
He's not telling me the truth
But I believe his lies

I can't let him go.
I think I love this guy
But I don't think this is love
I think it's a soul tie

I can't let him go
But he's already gone
He's got another girl
But I'm struggling to move on.

I've realized:

When sex gets involved
Things get a bit tricky
Physically, emotionally
Spiritually sticky

The mind wants to leave
But the body stays
Even if the person leaves

The thoughts won't go away.

Sex can make things blurry
The eyes can't see clearly anymore
She knows she needs to leave this man
But she can't see the door.

Sex can make you hold unto
Someone you need to leave
She knows that he is dangerous
But she can't seem to let go of his sleeve.

It's more than you think

The more I know
The more I grow
I learned that sex
Is more than "bang-bang" then go.

The more I know
The more I don't go with the flow
This thing called sex
Is more than in and out you know!

Sex is more than physical action
Sex is a spiritual transaction
Two shall become one flesh - the bible says this.
This is a covenant and your life will reflect this.

Exchange of spirits
Strong soul ties
You thought you could just finish
And say bye-bye.

You are now one with the person
Whoever they are
That's why you can't let any of these boys
Take you too far.

Sex has caused many people pain
Sex has made many insane
Because of sex - some are still paying
Ask him - he won't do that again.

This thing is no joke
 No, I don't want a one-night stand
No one should have access to you like that
Not even with their hand.

Left or right
Day or night
In the dark or light
You are not a loose woman
Tell him, "Get out of my sight".

If you want to marry me
Then you can wait for me
If you just want my body
Then get away from me.

God created sex; so sex is good
Within the boundaries of marriage –
I heard it's so, so good.

I'm saying all this because I care
I'm not trying to make you scared but aware about what's
going on out there.

Sorry for the strong words
I know this is intense
But I know you know what I'm talking about
You're nodding so this must make sense.

I'm tired of seeing my brothers fall
And my sisters taken advantage of
I've had enough of seeing this
Honestly, I've had enough. Enough is enough.

I'm speaking up
I'm preaching up
I'm teaching up
Daily - I'm reaching up.
For Grace,
Because I'm as tempted as you are

I don't want to be disqualified from this race.

God, please help me
I don't want to live a reckless life.
You know I'm single
Hurry up and show me my wife.

Just joking
That's not how to pray.
Relax. Chill. Enjoy the process.
You will be married one day.

It's a short ride

The last few days I've had different conversations
London, Manchester, different locations
The conversation had the same theme
Sex, pornography, and masturbation.

I group them all the same
Because they make you feel the same
In the moment you love it
Then it leaves you with a feeling of shame.

Ducking and diving
Hiding and skiving
Just to do it
Ooh'ing and Aah'ing.

This is a current plague
Attacking our generation
Playing with imaginations
What's the end of it all – depression.

In this sex theme park
The rides look lit but the end is dark
God wants you to enjoy sex for life
Not just a spark.

God created sex
And he said marriage is where to enjoy it
If you engage in it outside marriage
You will almost certainly regret it.

In the moment you feel good
But you will feel the pain later
When someone who said, "I love you"
Becomes your biggest hater.

God has boundaries
He is a God of order
But I understand
We live in a world of sexual disorder.

The world offers a quick fix
One night stand
Taking our youth by the hand
To fantasy land.

It's a short ride
That leaves them empty inside
Feeling used, abused
Then they go and hide.

I want to help our young people
Before it's too late
I am speaking like this because I care
I love you mate.

It's short but very long

Sin can only offer you short-term and short-lived smiles.
But it gives you sadness for many, many miles.
Sin is fast but it leaves you regretting the past.
The benefits are temporary but the problems can last for centuries.

Short term "pleasure"... Long term "pressure"
Short term "gain"... Long term "pain"
Short term "sweet"... Long term "heat"
Short term "highs"... Long term "cries"
Short term "feels good"... Long term "bad mood"
Short term "wet" ... Long term "regret"
Short term "great"... Long term "hate"
Short term "yes"... Long term "mess"
Short term "this is blessed"... Long term "this is stress"
Short term "Ahhhhhh"... Long term "Nahhhhhhhh"
Short term "chasing the pants"... Long term "chased by ants"
Short term "many ladies"... Long term "many babies"
Short term "many guys"... Long term "many lies"
Short term "we are having a good time"... Long term "what a waste of time"
Short term "shortcut"... Long term "long hurt"
Short term "fame"... Long term "shame"
Short term "claps"... Long term "slaps"
Short term "you're cool"... Long term "you're a fool"
Short term "class clown"... Long term "wearing a frown"
Short term "all over town"... Long term "down on the ground"
Short term "yes, yes, yes"... Long term "no, no, no"
Short term "having fun"... Long term "on the run"
Short term "first place"... Long term "disgrace"
Short term "winning the game"... Long term "no name".

The pleasure is short, but the pain is long.
In the short-term, the crowd may sing your song,

But in the long term, they won't sing along.

The benefits are brief, then it robs you like a thief
In the short term, people may sing your praise,
But in the long term, you will be erased.

Short term "my friends"... Long term "dead ends"
Short term "come along"... Long term "you don't belong"
Short term "good story"... Long term "bad memory"
Short term "you won"... Long term "you're gone"
Short term "you are the king"... Long term "you are nothing"
Short term "on top"... long term "dropped"

Sin can only offer you short-term and short-lived smiles;
But the pain is for many, many miles.
Sin is fast
But it leaves you regretting the past.
It's time to spin and throw sin in the bin;
When you run this race of life with God - you will win.

It's not a big deal

They say sex is no big deal
What's the fuss about?
It's just a bit of fun. We finish.
I go north - she goes south.

No big deal, right? Okay.

If it's not a big deal
Why are people addicted?

If it's not a big deal
Why are people arrested?

If it's not a big deal
Why does sex create life?

If it's not a big deal
Why are you cheating on your wife?

(Pause... no answer... longer pause...)

So, it is a big deal
But you're trying to play it down
Sex is one topic
That makes the world sit down

Put it in a film
Put it on TV
You will have an instant audience
Believe me!

Marketers know this too
They weave it into some adverts
If it's not a big deal
Then why are some people called perverts?

Sex is a topic

Many are silent about
Sex is a topic
Many comedians joke about

How often do you see it talked about seriously?
It's very rare
Some speakers hesitate
Because they're a bit scared.

It's difficult to preach about purity
When you're not trying to live it
It's like recommending a product
But you're not using it
"Eat your vegetables"
But you're not chewing it
"Stay away from temptation"
But you're running to it.

It's interesting how some churches place an emphasis on
relationship and sex issues
when its Valentine's day?
But sex is an issue affecting many people
Every single day.

It's no big deal... oh yes it is...

Here's another one,
If it's not a big deal
Why are most swear words sexual
Ever thought about that?

The one that rhymes with duck
The one that rhymes with stick
The one that rhymes with rock
The other one that rhymes with slick

The one that rhymes with pass
The one that rhymes with bread
These words are not part of my vocabulary

But I've heard them said.

If it's not a big deal, then why are break ups even more difficult when sex has been involved?

If sex is not a big deal, why are STDs such a big deal?

They were attracted to each other
One day, they got a little bit distracted
Unprotected sex. It's not a big deal though
It's only herpes they contracted.

It's only herpes...
WHAT?! That's a big deal!

I'm not playing

Every night different girl
All the ladies know his name
He's proud to be a playa
He says, "I'm winning this game".

Come on bro; I've asked around
This game gives you an appetizer of fame
But the main course is shame
At first - all gains
At last - all pains.

I asked some guys
Brothers, am I really missing out?
They said bro if you haven't started - don't!
It's not easy to come out.

They told me the truth
When you start, everything looks smooth
Different girls every week
But at the end - you will lose.

This game, I don't want to win
I don't even want to play
You "win" for 10 minutes
Then you lose all day.

That's not winning
You are sinning
That's not living
You are killing
You are harming your life
And hurting another man's wife.

This sex game is twisted

It's designed that way
The winner is the loser
That's why I don't want to play.

It's a dirty game

He told me step by step:

I tell her that and this; then I kiss
But my goal is to tick her body off my list
I enter the hole; Success!
I've put my pen in her book; now I can count it.

He said, I treat them nicely
I don't care if she's filthy, dirty or trash
After I finish with her
She orders the taxi; I give her the cash.

Sex is just a game for me
I don't even want to know her name
I'm a lion that cannot be tamed
But bro, are you not ashamed?

How can something so holy
Be made so cheap?
It's been made so shallow
But sex is very deep.

Sex has been reduced to a game
Sleep with the most and you win
No regard for God; no acknowledgement that
Sex outside marriage is a sin.

Some people want to be saved
But from sex addiction; they don't want to be free
They say: Lord heal me from my other problems
But leave this sex one for me.

If it is your will, heal me later or never
God, you choose

But I'm enjoying this game too much
I'm winning and I don't want to lose.

If you are playing this game
I learned something – I must tell
You are dancing at a very risky place
You are dancing at the gate of hell.

Don't abuse God's grace
It's not an excuse to do wrong
You are playing with fire
Eternity is very long.

Who's playing who?

Today,
Both genders play
Men play
Women play
It goes both ways.

Guys, check this out
You think you're the one moving to her
She already moved to you.
You think you saw her first
Ha! She already saw you.
She moved to a place
So you could see her
Bro, women are very clever.

While you are thinking about what to say
She already has a reply
You are trying to make it sound true
She already has a lie.

The guy thinks; I'll hit and run
In the morning - I'm gone!
But she has already targeted him
As the future father of her son.

There are a lot of professional actors out there
Who are not in Hollywood;
They're in your neighborhood
And they're up to no good.

Whatever games guys play
Women play too
You think you are playing her
Nah bro, she's playing you.

People say guys don't marry bad girls
They only date them.

Date and dash
Use and abuse
When it's time to leave
Any excuse.

But who's playing who?

They say some guys are trash
But some girls are too
Nowadays you need more than your eyes
To separate the lie from the truth.

Where are the good girls?
Where are the good guys?
They are around somewhere
But you need to open your spiritual eyes.

Even in Church
You can't trust all you see
God bless you, Praise the Lord, Hallelujah
It's all learned vocabulary.

What are you doing?

I'm a virgin
Everybody knows
What does she look like?
I don't know
Never seen a woman naked in real life
From her head to her toes
I've had opportunities though
But nothing happened - I froze.

I was face to face with her
I heard a voice saying: WHAT ARE YOU DOING?!
Do you know what this means?
Honestly, WHAT ARE YOU DOING?!

Have you forgotten your values?
Have you forgotten who you are?
Whatever pleasure you are about to get,
It's done after an hour.

Even if you take a shower
You can't wash the guilt away
Wounds can heal
But trust me, this scar will stay.

What would Jesus think of this?
After he washed your sins away
Don't take grace for granted
It's not an excuse to play.

You've been told many times
You've been taught about the consequences
Life is simple
It's people that make complex sentences.

This is a trap
Wrapped in sugar and glitter
Once all the fun is done
Your life will be very bitter.

So, get up and run
Tie your shoe lace
If your dad saw you here,
What would you say to his face?

You're an example
People look up to you
If you do this
They will do it too.

Holiness gives you boldness
No need to hide
Inside and outside - everywhere
You can be the same guy.

You know you are clean
So you can keep a straight face
Check all the records
You won't find a trace.

How did you find yourself here?
What were you planning to do?
There are many traps in the world
But they don't have to catch you.

Guys - let's fix up

In life you grow, in life you know
In life you earn, in life you learn
My mind is tough now
I've had enough now
What I'm about to say you might not like
So if you want to - turn this off now.

We used to look up to those guys because of how many girls
they had
But now I know better
That lifestyle is actually sad
Counting girls like coins is not good - it's actually bad.

How many girls have you had?
How many pants have you taken off?
He said, "about twenty
After each one - I take off".

Body count, body count
What's your amount?
One, two
Twenty, thirty
Me and you both know - that's kind of dirty.

He said, "He's got stamina".
He's got the power, so he goes around tapping
This doesn't impress me; I might be in the audience
But I won't be clapping.

Guys, we need to stop making life about banging girls
If we fix up - we can actually fix this world

God designed us to be the head of the home
Some of us care more about getting head than getting home.

Stay committed to your woman
And leave all those side chicks alone.

We need to take responsibility
We need to fix up
There is a generation growing up
And they are looking at us.

They are learning from us
Brothers, it's true
If they were looking for a role model
Ask yourself, would you want them to look at you?

Ladies – keep your knickers on

He was treating her like she was the one
He said there are no other girls in his life; zero, none.
She felt special then she gave him some
He put on his seat belt for safety - the condom.
That's all he wanted - a bit of fun
As soon as it was done - he was gone.
She thought she met the one
But she woke up next to no one
Same old story, back to square one.

Was she in the wrong?
Some say yes, some say no.
She should have waited; I think so.

You see, time reveals whether he is real or fake
Time reveals if he is here to give or just take.
Time will reveal whether he is cheap meat or the original
steak
Time will tell whether he is one of those who stay
Or one of those weak ones that break.

I'm a guy and I'm telling you today
It doesn't matter what he says,
Don't be in a hurry to serve him your body on a tray.
Many who did regret that day
They came back to tell us
"Wait till your wedding day;
The marriage route is the right way."

"I'm so embarrassed," she said,
"Everyone thinks my standards are low.
I thought I knew this guy, but obviously I didn't know
How do I get out of this situation? Where do I go?"

I know one way, but it is very narrow
It's called the Purity road
I'm on it now and there is less stress and sorrow.
Jesus leads the way; we just follow
He teaches us every day so we can have a brighter tomorrow.

Easy come, easy go

Hey girls,
If you make it easy for him
He will come and go
He'll have you tonight
But there's no tomorrow.
As soon as day comes
Off you go.

Can we be friends?
I don't think so.
Why?
He says she's the kind of girl
That can't tell a guy no.
Whatever he does
She just goes with the flow.
Look at her clothes
Nothing's hidden, it's all on show.

By the way she dresses
I don't think she's a keeper
She's looks like a sleeper,
One of those girls
If you're bored - just beep her.
Her dress shows it all
And that's how guys see her
Her dress says it all
And that's how guys treat her.
That's why guys want to meet her
For only one night,
Then 'see you later'.

Is there any commitment today?

Some are hard to get
Because their assets are deep
She values herself as a person
She said, "I'm not cheap."

Some are easy to get
Easy to sleep
We just met
And she wanted to let me peep.

This was too easy
Too easy to win
That area is private
But she wanted to let me in.

When the journey to the bed is easy
It gets you thinking
This kind of person could leave me tomorrow
Without even blinking.

If she can fall for me after 10 minutes
She could probably slip for another man
I didn't play my best game
And I won this girl with one hand

Easy come
Easy go
Today "yes"
Tomorrow "no"

What about the guys?

Telling little lies
Wandering eyes

When it's time for commitment
They say goodbye.

You're right
There are 'playas' out there
Playing everywhere
As long as there is a field of girls
They'll play anywhere.

In their game
The goal is the bed
If they can't score between the legs
They're okay with head.

It's really sad
What our world has come to
People are just looking for people
To get aroused and go through.

They say it's just a bit of fun
No strings attached
But when you've had sex - You are one
It's hard to detach.

You have built a house with someone
And you think you won't see them again
It's a spiritual connection
It will replay in your brain.

It makes some insane
It brings some a lot of pain
Their spirit wants to leave
But their body still remains.

To heal the pain
They keep looking and looking

Sleeping and sleeping
Again and again.

You are not like them
You are a person of value
Ladies and gentlemen
Don't throw away your virtue.

It's so complicated
How do I break free?
Jesus is the answer
He is the one helping me.

Too easy

She was too easy.
She served him her body
He didn't work hard to eat
He's bored now
He's looking for fresh meat.

I'm just saying
As a guy
"Easy girls"
Don't seem to catch my eye.

At least let him say something
Something a little sweet
Her knees are already on the floor
She's swept off her feet.

Easy come; easy go
Ladies, if you give it to him easy today
He'll be gone tomorrow.

Men value what they work for
Men value what they fought for
If you sell yourself cheap
He will use you and leave you on the floor.

In his mind, if she can do this to me
She can do it to another guy - she's easy
No way am I making her my 'wifey'.

Guys; it works the same way
You think you have game
But women also play.

She said,

"This is not husband material
He's just a boy
I'll play with him
I'll use him like a toy."

We all have to look at ourselves
Men and women
What kind of example are we setting for our children?

One night stand
One night sit
"I'll let him do whatever," she said.
"I think he's fit."

One night sit
One night stand
"I'll let her do whatever", he said.
"She's got magic hands."

This casual sex lifestyle
Is not the way to go
You don't have to say yes
You can say no.

Be a man of dignity
Be a woman of virtue
Respect yourself, please
You are people of value.

Can we wait babe?

Babe, let us lie down
I want to show you how much I love you
I want to twist and turn you
Caress and impress you
Love on you and give all I am to you.

(She's very impressed)

Do you really love me? She asked.
Yes, he replies.
Do you really really love me?
Yes I really really really love you, he replies.
As in love, cherish, value, and honour me?

(He starts singing)

You are my African queen, my everything. You are my African
queen; I want to show you with my ding a ling a ling.

(She laughs)

You are so cute. So talented. So desirable.
I'm so blessed to have a man like you who is interested in me
and not just my body.

(He nods repeatedly) Yes. Yes. Yes.

Therefore I know you will respect my decision for us to wait.
I will not open my gates for you until the wedding day.
What if my name is Bill?
No money can buy this honey.
This treasure is beyond measure
And I won't give it out for casual pleasure.

I know you are attracted to me
I am attracted to you too
But let's wait till we both have rings
Then it's just me and you.

No shame, no fear
On the bed, on the chair
Over here - over there
Just me and you my dear.

All day, all night
When it's dark and in the light
With pillows, under the sheets
Our bodies generating holy heat.

(He nods repeatedly) Yes. Yes. Yes.

Looking forward to it, she said
It's going to be great
But for now
We wait

Can you wait babe?

He's too fast

Us guys...

We are eager to start but not willing to stay.
We want to plant the seed and eat the fruit on the same day.
If we could meet her, date her, and propose today – some of us
would do it...
But it doesn't work that way.

Ladies; he may be in a rush, but don't be rushed.
He's got big boy words and big boy bars but don't get swept off
your feet.
He looks cool today but this guy might be heat.
I know he's neat – but don't let him make your heart skip a
beat.
Go home, think, pray, take a seat.
I'm telling you this as a guy;
Because some guys see girls as a piece of meat.

Some of us guys can get a bit excited at times.
A comedian said guys have two brains –
The one in our head can be practical
But the one in our boxers can be insane.
So if he's going a bit too fast – tell him to relax
That's all I'm saying.

She learned her lesson

The building lasted long because it had a strong foundation.
I think a solid marriage is built by removing sex from the
dating equation.
Correct me if I'm wrong – I'm open to correction, but I think
sex really changes the quality of conversations.
Before it was vision - what is your life purpose and mission?
Now they are having sex; they only talk about the next
position.

Hi... what's the next position we can try... after sex he packs up
and says bye, then I hug my teddy and cry. He still loves me
though – it's a lie!
She said, "We used to talk about deep things – he was with me
when times were low.
Now I feel he just uses me for pleasure – after he's done, he
gets up and goes –
There's no connection and I know he knows – I regret this
path that I chose."

Our relationship started getting dry, the spark we had
gradually died.
Before I knew it – he texted me saying, I don't think this is
working – goodbye.
What do I do? I cried, I tried to make it work – I tried.
Was it something I did, or something he did?
No, it was sex that created the divide.

Now I tell my girls to decide – If you choose to have casual
sex... Honey let's talk;
Let me tell you about the other side.
First it's pleasure, then it's pain. I've learned my lesson; I'm
not doing that again.

I'm waiting till marriage – you might think that's insane, but God instructed us to do this because it leads to more gain and less pain.

Access denied

He tried to penetrate
But she closed the gate
I'm not that kind of girl
Don't try it with me mate.

He tried to make a move again
She said, "Stop it."
I'm not that kind of girl anymore
"Honestly, I'll chop it."

Cooked, grilled or baked
How do you like it?
The last guy that attempted
I almost fried it.

That was the last time he ever tried it.

Because of one night

One night can ruin your one life... Is it worth it?
It might be "fun," but do you want to spend the rest of your life on the run?

It might be "fun," but when it's done, everywhere you go, will you have your back turned?

I tell people the options and the outcomes, so they can decide whether they really want some.

Why is he not looking up? Well, after he "turned up", he got a full cup – a full cup of stress.
Now his life is a mess; I bet he regrets that night when he took off her dress.

Play in the night, you may pay in the day. Cause trouble in the night, it may come for you in the day.
Certain things in life are not easy to wash away.

He doesn't have the boldness to show his face,
Because of what he did, he feels like a disgrace.

Enjoy the night, but don't forget there is day,
What you planted last night, you will reap today, tomorrow or some other day.

At the end of the day, it's your choice.
I know you are a wise person; I don't need to raise my voice.

A wise person only needs one caution; they take instruction, accept correction and that's why they avoid destruction.

Are you his girlfriend or wife?

My sisters, consider this...

Doing tasks that are not on your job description is nice
But the employer doesn't have to pay.
Similarly
Doing wife duties as a girlfriend
Doesn't mean he will marry you one day.

Please also note:

Giving him sex quick
And hoping he will stick is a risk
He may get tired of your flavor
And move to another dip.

If you give him everything
There is no more surprise
So don't complain
When he has wandering eyes.

In a man's mind:

She already cooks for me.
She already cleans after me.
She already sleeps with me.
Why do I need to marry her?
I like it just the way it is.
If it's not broken; why change it?

I'm living my best life
And she's not even my wife
She does everything
And it didn't cost me a ring.

But I hope she knows there are no guarantees
If she starts acting up or messing up
I'll find another girl to meet my needs.

Love then Marriage then Sex

L.M.S.
Love then Marriage then Sex
I think this is God's order
It works out for the best.

It's up to you
Don't say you were not told
This casual sex lifestyle
Is making many young people look old.

But I love her though
And I want to show her how much
You are playing with fire
Please don't touch.

Sex is not love
Love is not sex
Since you love her so much - marry her
This is God's best.

God knows you
He is your maker
He gave instructions to help not hurt you
He is your Creator.

I'm not ready to marry
But I like sleeping with Barry
It's up to you
If a baby comes - you will carry!

Mind your business
He's my boyfriend
I've seen it all before
I know how this story ends.

Here comes your son
Why are you sad?
Where's Barry gone?
He doesn't want to be a dad.

No hurry to marry

Parent talking to their child...

You're not in a hurry to marry
Because you are enjoying the benefits already
You live with her, you sleep with her
You even bought a dog and a telly.

That's why some young people feel old
You did the opposite of what you were told
Now you're a single mom and you have a son
Pushing a buggy around in the cold.

There's no one to blame
I know this is harsh – but it's true
You did the act and now you face the facts
What are you going to do?

When I was telling you this before
You refused to understand
I only wanted the best for you
I carried you in the palm of my hand.

There nothing we can do now
This is not the time to sob
Get your laptop; let's work on your CV
You need to get a job.

Why?
Oh, you don't know what you've done
Son, you have a son
He is your responsibility – you have to take ownership
Don't even try to run.

I will repeat my original instruction

To anyone that is willing to hear
Whether you do it or not – it's up to you
I am saying this because I care.

My son, until you are married
Don't show her the 'weapon' you carry
My daughter, until you are married
Please, don't open your legs for any Tom, Dick, or Harry.

Run Back

There's so much temptation
Everywhere distraction
Focus on your race
Life's an individual competition.

All runners start
But not all end
Some followed sin
And their life took a bend.

He was looking forward
Now his head's downward
The devil told him, "Don't go back to Church.
You're a coward."

It doesn't matter how long it's been
I know you've been falling into sin
Turn to God
By His Grace, you can still win.

Don't run away, run to God,
Get down on your knees
I know you feel trapped
But He's got the keys.

Run to God,
He's got the Light
One word from Him,
Your life will be bright.
Stay with Him
He'll change your life.
I know you've been going wrong
But He will lead you right.

The guy who changed my life

I could but I won't
Not because I can't
I can.
I choose not to
Because I understand
The man
Who allowed nails to be put in his hands
For my freedom.
After knowing this, how can I do this?
That's wickedness.

I cannot do what you do
Because I know someone you don't know
No disrespect. No pride. No arrogance.
But if you knew this guy -
You probably wouldn't go.

What about grace?
Grace!
Some use as an excuse to choose to do abuse.
Many teachings out there but
I am not confused.
My relationship with this guy;
I don't want to lose.

Who is this guy though?

From darkness to light
He changed my life.

From blindness to sight
He changed my life.

From fear of the night

He changed my life.

Who is this guy?
Jesus Christ.

Temptation gave me correction

Based on a true life story...

Ike: (falling into temptation)
Temptation: What are you doing?
Ike: (stops)
Temptation: Aren't you that Christian motivational guy?
Ike: (pause) I am... (walks away)

I had an erection
Temptation gave me correction.
She reminded me of my heavenly connection.
I stood at attention.
I felt like a school child who was getting sent to detention.
Ashamed. One word - I couldn't mention
Temptation was right...
I stopped and changed direction.

I was getting a bit too excited and carried away
She reminded me who I was: "Are you okay?"
Aren't you that guy that posts Christian motivational stuff on social media every day?

Lesson learned:
You can live your life in such an openly godly way
That even when you are going the wrong way,
Temptation will remind you to read your Bible and pray.

"Temptation, why are you helping me?
That is very strange."
I'm not really trying to help you
I'm just checking if you've changed.
People like you are normally out of my range.

Don't be ashamed. This is a good thing.

This shows you are doing something right.
This means that even darkness knows that you are the light.
This is just a reminder to keep your light shining bright.

Consider this a wake-up call
This has shown you that even the strongest Christian can
easily fall.
Whoever thinks they are standing tall, should check, check and
keep checking,
So they don't fall.
If Jesus was tempted, it will happen to us all.

Women are my weakness

Our enemy is clever
He uses your weakness to tempt you
If you fall for women easily
He'll employ many seductive ones
To pass by you; to contact you;
To have long conversation,
"Come let's go on vacation"
Divert you from your destination
Mission accomplished.
He has succeeded to distract you.

A woman can be a man's best friend.
A woman can also make a man bend.
It doesn't matter how "powerful"
"Educated" "serious" "holy" "Christian"
A woman's touch - the end.

Some men won't lie.
Steal – No, he won't do that sin.
But send an attractive woman in
Bingo. You've got him.

If this is you
I'm in your shoes
I don't know what to say
Apart from tell you what I do

Look unto God
Pray for Grace
"Lord, you gave me these urges
help me to keep them in their right place – marriage".

Turn it off

I need to tell you something son
Some of these "photos" are actually porn
When you see them - turn
If you need to - run
Turn it off before you're turned on.

It's just a picture, they say
That's how it starts
Some of this and some of that
Before you know it - you're hooked
No going back.

Son you have to choose:
If you want to be good - be good
If you want to be bad - be bad
If you want to be happy - be happy
If you want to be sad - be sad
If you want to be hot - be hot
If you want to be cold - be cold
But don't say you were not told.

This porn thing has messed many people up
The young and the old
The black and the white
It's wrong; it's not right
I love you son
That's why I'm telling you this tonight.

I don't watch it

Do you watch...?

No, I stopped watching it...

The show comes on late
So I watched it before bed
Dirty thoughts, dirty dreams
It was messing with my head

The producers are clever
They know how to keep your attention
Every episode ends with a suspension
Tension... different dimensions
The viewers can't wait to watch the next session

It's interesting
I'm not going to lie
But it was messing with my head
I needed to protect my eyes

The eyes are the windows
To the mind
What you put in
Is what you will find

I'm in the inspiration business
I need clarity
Also, I want to live a life of sexual purity
And that show wasn't helping me
So I stopped lying to myself
And I switched off the TV.

Big industry causing big issues

It's a big industry
Causing really big issues
Porn is wasting many lives
And wasting many tissues

The eyes are the windows
To the mind
Many people have eyes
But porn has made them blind

They can't really see anymore
Their perception has changed
Can't look at a person
Without seeing them unchanged

Naked
No clothes on
Everything is a trigger for sex
Even a tampon

He sees the color red
Thoughts fill his head
He can't wait to watch sex, sex, sex
On his bed, bed, bed!

The eyes have seen too much nudity
All day; all night watching obscenity
It has twisted their mentality
They've lost touch with reality

It's a pity.

Youth should have strength
You are young - it's your prime
Porn is sucking their energy
And wasting their time

Okay now you're married
This is your wife - the real thing
Go ahead but he's confused.
He can't do anything

The thing can't stand
He has no feeling
Erectile dysfunction
He needs healing

His pen used to write
But it ran out of ink
He wasted it on fake paper
Flushed his children down the sink

Don't say "they're too young"
"Oh, they're just youth"
We have to be honest
And tell them the truth... early!

Because the world is not
Asking about their age
The world is encouraging them
To keep scrolling down the page.

I know sex sells
but you don't have to buy into the temptation.
My objective is to share a different perspective
with this generation

I have to physically, spiritually
and regularly break myself away
I'm free and I want to lead others to freedom today.

Temptation in Isolation

Did God really tell you
Not to eat from the tree?
The snake tricked Eve
Now he's trying to trick me

Go on... watch it
You're in isolation
There's nothing wrong with porn
And a little masturbation.

God understands
It's a global situation
Coronavirus
It's affecting every nation

Tell God it's research
You're working on that book
A few videos won't hurt
Just take a look

If it's a work computer
Use your phone
No one will catch you
You're all alone

Everyone is doing it
It's not a mystery
After you watch it
Delete your history

The same snake that tempted Eve
back in the day
Is still working over-time
Tricking Christians today.

He's a liar, a fraud,
A sneaky little rat

He'll try his best in this season
Please don't fall for that.

He wants to settle down

He was chasing women all over town
His type was a brunette or a brown.
Buying anything to get them;
Tops, bags, blouses, and gowns.
This lifestyle left him with a frown
Money down
Looking back, he realized that he was a clown.
He woke up one morning
And he said, "Enough is enough;
I need to settle down."

He wants to settle down.
He wants a wife – a good woman
First things first;
Give up all those side 'tings'
And occasional 'flings'
Because they will stop you
From seeing the real thing.

Totally?
Yes, totally
Physically, Spiritually and Emotionally
Mentally, Financially, Absolutely and Completely
Detached.
You can't go forward if you are attached to the past.
If you start this new race with the old weights
You will finish last - again.
Rewind the pain.
Money down the drain.
Do you want that again?
"Never!" he said.

Since you said you wanted a wife
You need to give up the old ways – the old life.

Old things are passed way - all things are new
It's one thing to want a wife
It's another thing for her to want you.

So, preparing you is the best you can do.
The way you were before, if you were a woman
Would you say "I do" to you?
No.

You were a liability before
I know you want to be an asset.
When it comes to marriage
You have to put all your eggs in one basket.

Buy before you try

Some people say try before you buy.

But what if they try and don't buy?
How will that make you feel?
Sorry this body is not for trying;
First, you have to sign the deal!

What's the deal? Marriage.
Together forever
Can I bring her back?
You mean divorce?

Are you thinking about that already?

It's not healthy to marry
With divorce in mind
Some people are looking for
The smallest reason they can find

There's no return policy
But you can keep the receipt
Marriage is not a drive thru
You have to settle down and eat.

You can try with your mouth
By talking, by walking
By dating, no rubbing,
No sexy nothing.

Haven't you heard of a test-drive?
I want to see if we fit
I want to see if we're compatible
I want to practice technique.

Practice technique
You must be joking
My daughter is not for trial and error
What are you smoking?

There are a lot of sweet talkers
Who promise they will buy
"I'm committed to you babe
Honestly, no lies!"

In their mind
They just want to try
It's a hit and run mission
It's a sexual drive-by.

They take advantage
And then say bye.
A cold-hearted attack
They leave their victim to cry.

We don't believe in try before you buy
You need to buy before you try
My baby girl is not one of those chicks
You can use and leave on the side.

Get your hands off her knees!
Get your hands off her thighs!
You don't have my blessing yet!
You haven't even paid the bride price.

Young man,
Put your 'marry' where your mouth is
Then you can have all of her
However you like it.

What if I don't like it?

And I don't like her moves
Keep learning together
You will both improve.

Please note:
If you think you can try a couple of girls
Then come to my daughter to settle down - you're a clown!
We have standards here;
And we won't drop them down.
She's a queen
And she won't take off her crown.
Remember my words when you go into town.

Pick one

Hey guy, have you found one?
Done. Time to close my eyes.
Other girls?
I don't want none.

Don't you want some?
One, two or three?
I will focus on this one
That's how God intended it to be.

Time on the phone
Time alone
This is the flesh of my flesh
And the bone of my bone.

Scatter your seeds
Explore and be free
Play the field
I disagree.

Pick one out of them all
Do it all for that one
Not everyone or anyone
Invest all your energy on that one.

One sex partner.
No next.
We make it work.
She's my best.

One man.
One woman.
One marriage.
One picture.

One future.
One vision.
In agreement.
No division.

Two brains
One head.
Two people
One bed.

Two players
One team.
Two thinkers
One dream.

One love
One family.
One life
We're happy.

One woman

One woman is enough for me.
One.
I don't want any others.
None.

They say protect yourself.
Watch yourself.
What you need to do is
Stop picking up women like food from the shelf.

Do you like this one?
Have that one
Go on take one
I told you before, I don't want none.

I'm good thanks
I'm okay.
Men like me are waiting for the wedding day
Then I'll play.

No shame, no rules
We will both be students learning "how to".
After that, we will both be the teacher
We will teach each other all the moves.

I'm choosing this path
I've seen the benefit.
My friends who had sex before marriage
Told me they regret it.

They said to me,
"Yo Ike, I wish we could change seats.
It was cool when I was doing it
But now I'm feeling the heat.

In the sun,
We were having lots of fun.
But the story took a twist
Crash and burn
Now, I'm on the run."

"Learn from me," he said.
"Don't live that life.
Take your mind off her and the bed
Focus on your vision instead.

I'll be honest with you
The body wants to
The Spirit said, 'Don't do'.
You are not ready
You are biting more than you can chew.

This meal is not for today
Don't worry! When you're married
You can eat it every day
Don't eat tomorrow's food today
Sex tastes better after the wedding day."

This is your life
She is your wife
You can do it any time
Before breakfast or after work at five.

Nothing to be ashamed of, nothing to lose.
I told you before
When you're married
There are no rules.
Actually, there might be – it's up to both of you.

Satisfy each other

Be ready, be available.
Actually there is one rule
Don't eat at another woman's table.

It doesn't matter how you feel
Don't eat a strange woman's meal.
Even if she's hot and spicy
Don't eat. You already signed a deal.

Go back home
Enjoy your wife.
Dive into her breasts
But not with a fork and knife.

Okay, jokes aside
Did you know that God created you?
Inside and outside
He created sex too
And He gave us the Bible as a guide.

Some people might be thinking
I've done a lot and I can't take it back.
My life is a mess
I'm ashamed of my past.

Two words for you: Come back
No need to hide.
Come back to God and surrender your life
Swallow your pride.
God is gracious and merciful
It doesn't matter what you've done;
He can let it slide.

You don't need to explain
You don't need to justify.
Jesus divided his body

So you can live free and multiply.

Jesus paid the price
So we can live, love and laugh.
When you follow His ways
You have chosen the good path.

You crashed, you burned
But the good news is you turned.
You turned back to God
So, what's the biggest lesson you learned?

Respect yourself
You are a somebody.
You are God's creation
You're not a nobody.
And even if everyone is doing it
You don't have to sleep with anybody.

Do I still have to wait?

I was asked a question
It's simple but sticky
I want to get your opinion
I'm not trying to be tricky.

I want to get your point of view
If you were in his shoes
What would you do?

He said...

"Our wedding was supposed to be in April
Because of the coronavirus - we moved the date
I was looking forward to having sex with my wife
Does this mean we still have to wait?

Technically were not "married"
Public gatherings are banned
Obviously this wasn't our plan
So do you think God will understand?"

COVID-19 has delayed his wedding reception
This is a very unique situation
Should he wait
or proceed towards penetration?

Survey says: Wait!

Wait

If you think she is the one
Wait for her
If you think he is the one
Wait for him.
I know many say it's the 21st century but
Sex outside of marriage is still a sin.

Just because you have it
It doesn't mean you have to use it.
With great power comes great responsibility
You don't have to take that opportunity.

The world says:
Slide on the durex – it's a normal thing to do.
But you are worth more than all that
God paid a huge price for you.

We are surrounded by temptations
Chests, breasts, all kind of tests.
It's easy to fall, but I encourage you to stand
Whatever your past is - that's gone
God can make you a new man.
If you want to surrender your life to God, please raise your
hand.

My past - He wiped away
I've forgotten about what happened yesterday.
My total focus is now
How can I glorify God with my body today?

Talk to your body

I like women - many
But I want to marry one - not many
This truth helps me calm down
When my body wants to sleep with many.

I like women - many
Hailey, Lucy, and Jenny
God, can I have all 3?
You can but it's not free.

The consequences have a price
Have you counted the cost?
If you want to play this game
Son, you've already lost.

It's impossible to win
When you are playing with sin
You will get beaten and battered
And put in the bin.

Tell your body to calm down
"Yo penis, keep your cool"
I know you're a wise man
You're not a fool.

The male organ can be stubborn.
Keep talking to him
I didn't say hold him
Because that could lead to sin.

Keep talking to your body
"Calm down"
Whenever he stands up
Tell him to "sit down."

Not now
This is not my wife
If I act on your urges
It will mess up my life.

It is natural to be turned on
And not know how to turn off
I didn't say sexual purity is easy
I understand – it can be tough.

Erections happen
It can happen at any place or time
But you must keep reminding your raging organ
"This woman is not mine."

There is a place and time for this
There is a place and time for sex
We could have it now casually
But this is not God's best.

I know she's fine
But let's not cross this line
Let us honour God
Marriage is a beautiful design.

He made a vow

Addicted, how do I stop?
He didn't know how
Later, he discovered the power of a vow
He said: "God if I watch it again - kill me"
Guess what?
The addiction stopped instantly
It's been 7 years
Since he watched pornography.

I also know someone
Who was faced with temptation
This temptation was on another dimension
He said "a vow is the only solution."
He got on his knees and prayed
"God, if I sleep with this girl
give me AIDS."

AIDS is related to HIV
Some people are thinking
These kind of prayers – seriously?
Yes! You can't treat temptation casually
You have to kill it or it will kill you eventually.

Surrender your sexuality

Many of us want to be saved
But we don't want to be totally free
We pray "God, help me with these problems
But leave this sex addiction for me."

Lord, I'm winning this game
And I don't want to quit
I'm not going to lie
I'm enjoying it.

Like numbers
I'm counting these chicks
Bang two bodies at a time
Look at my list and tick.

Last night Rachel
Tonight Leonie
I've got choices
I've got many.

You may think you're winning
But you are sinning
This game kills its players
I'm not even joking.

The game is twisted
Perverted by the enemy
I've had opportunities
To tap a girl next to me.

The game is twisted
You play then you pay
The winners are the losers
That's why I don't play.

He said,
"Sex is fun though
It eliminates my boredom
I call a chick at random
Then I strap on the condom.

I'm handsome
They want some."
No. You are a slave, a prisoner
You need a ransom.

Jesus came for our freedom
He wants to set us free
Surrender all to him
Including your sexuality.

He cares and He understands everything
Even our desire to use our hands
He was tempted as we all are
He lived here as a human.

Single, Serving, and Searching

I'm single, serving and searching
Just so you know - I'm a virgin.
I know you're thinking - Wow
What's this I'm hearing?

Sorry that was direct
But I say this with all due respect.
If you're looking for a guy with "experience"
That's not me - you can go to the next.

It doesn't make me less of a man
I'm telling you, just so you know.
I've had opportunities left and right
But I said, "Sorry, no."

28 years old
Confident, calm and bold.
God bought this body with a high price
I cannot be cheaply sold.

I'm telling you early so you know
So you won't think I'm something that I'm not.
I don't have my house yet, I don't have a car yet
A vision is all I've got.

That's me plain and simple,
1, 2, 3 - that's triple.
I have nothing to hide; I'm the same guy inside
I can show you every pimple.

God will guide me to my bride
God will guide her to her groom.
After the marriage, we shut the door
Whatever we do stays in the room.

Don't hate on any of your mates
Your time is coming soon.
Do what's right - your future is bright
Just like a Sunday afternoon.

I know it's been a while
Hold unto God as your guide.
Life is simple; enjoy it while you're single
Go for a swim and slide.

My relationship with women

I can talk to you
I can walk with you
I can sit with you
I can stand with you
I can laugh with you
I can cry with you
I can pray with you
I can stay with you
I can play with you
I can spend all night and day with you
I can do all these things but...

I will not enter you.
What do you mean?
I have no ulterior motive.
What do you mean?
I will not penetrate you.
What do you mean?
I will not have sex with you.

What if you like me and I like you?
You are not my wife. I will not have sex with you.

I choose not to use

She was loose
But I chose not to use
She was loose
She was giving out free juice.

She was very loose as a teenager
Got tighter in her twenties
She's no longer dirty-minded
I still talk to her - she's about thirty.

I had a chance to smash and grab
She was known around town
I saw the queen inside her
And I helped her to find her crown.

If you take advantage of them when they are down
They will remember you when they get up
She will always remember you
As the guy who messed her up.

Imagine if I took advantage of her
When she was loose
Whenever she saw me
She would remember the abuse.

You will remember those who kicked you down
You will remember those who picked you up
I want to be remembered as the guy
Who had a chance but didn't get on top.

Brothers; choose not to use her
Even if she's loose - don't abuse her
Her soul is torn; you don't have to make it wider
Be a good guy; bring out the queen inside her.

No strings attached

I don't want it on my conscience
That I made her miss eternity.

I don't want it on my conscience
That I stole her virginity.

I don't want it on my conscience
That's the guy that manipulated me.

I don't want it on my conscience
That's the guy that attached himself to me.

I don't want to be ducking and diving
Avoiding some girls in a meeting
I want to walk with my head up
I don't want to be known for cheating.

I don't want to be that guy
I don't want to be that guy
I don't want to be that guy
That makes girls cry.

I don't want to be that dude
I don't want to be that dude
I don't want to be that dude
That enters a room and creates a negative mood.

One girl hated me
I didn't even know it
Whenever my name came up
She said she wanted to vomit.

Eventually she told me why
"You were leading me on to no end

Your actions were showing more
But you say we are just friends."

I understood my wrongs
I apologised and apologised
I was sending mixed messages
I only just realized.

There was a lot of tension
But I learned a major lesson
A guy can move on easier
But the girl may go into depression.

I don't want it on my conscience
That I made her miss school
I don't want it on my conscience
That I made her drown herself in the pool.

I don't want it on my conscience
That somebody's life was damaged by mine
I don't want it on my conscience
That I'm the guy that made her cross the line.

I don't want to be tied down
To any living or dead soul
No strings attached
This is one of my goals.

The Unsexy Generation

We are the unsexy generation.
We are a chosen generation.
A holy nation.
Marriage is the destination for sexual satisfaction.
We are driving straight ahead.
We are not stopping at any station.
We are not stopping for masturbation.
We are not stopping to watch babe station.
We won't divert for a sin vacation.
No, these are the distractions that are corrupting this generation.
We are a chosen generation.
We made a decision.
To delay gratification.
A separation from worldly obsession.
A lifestyle of sanctification.
We run from temptation.
We wait in anticipation.
We have a hope and expectation.
The Lord is our light and our salvation.
Marriage is the destination for sexual satisfaction.
Husband and wife interaction. It's for life - no graduation.
In obedience to God – there is no condemnation.
We are the unsexy generation.

Warning; your babies are old

While you're thinking it's too early
You are getting too late
You may think they are too young
Ha! These kids nowadays are old.

This is generation fast
This is not the time to take it slow
They know more than you think they know.

But he's just a baby
In age - maybe
Some of these kids are old people
In baby bodies.

He's just a child
So you think
Your child is wild
Did you know that he drinks?

He's a good boy
So you say
How do you know that?
You speak to him less than 10 minutes a day.

Assumptions
Is the mother of destruction
Your child is still a child
They need your instruction.

Instructions, restrictions
Boundaries and rules
When they grow up
They will look back and say "thank you."

Education starts at home
Including the sex talk;
Don't assume they know it
Don't leave them alone.

If you don't teach your kids inside
Someone will teach them outside.
If you don't teach them the truth
Someone will teach them the lie.

They will live rough outside the house
But you won't know
Because inside - they are quiet as a mouse.

My good boy
My source of joy
Here's more money
Go out and enjoy.

You don't know him at all
He is living in sin
If you don't help him
Your "good boy" will turn into trash
And end up in the bin.

On the purity road

You need a holy GPS when navigating these worldly roads;
Especially at night time.

"Road slippery
Temptation ahead
Don't stop at the sex junction
Take the next exit
And turn back as soon as possible.
I will direct you to a better path."

GPS Navigation aka The Holy Spirit

I'm on the holy highway
Marriage is the destination
I will not follow signs that say
"This road leads to temptation."

This purity road is narrow
It requires discipline and dedication
Sacrifice and determination
But the end is satisfaction.

When I arrive
I will give God glory and adoration
It's not by my power
But the power of His resurrection.

From the beginning of creation
He knew me in my mother's belly
I am God's child
I can't give my body to pornography.

Life will send different tests and temptations
Yes, there will be hard examinations

May God help me to pass with a distinction
Then marriage will be my graduation.

The temptation doesn't stop after marriage
I know that for sure
May God give me the wisdom, grace and strength
To do what's right and pure.

It's not time to eat yet

(**Warning:** A lot of symbolic language)

Let the relationship marinate in the spices of thyme
You are coming together like salt and pepper
Deliberately invest in the cooking process.
All hands on deck; no nibbling of the neck.

Soon, you will be eating the same meat
Cooked in different ways and positions
So don't be in a haste to taste
It will be yours forever one day.

Talk more; touch less
Don't worry about what is inside her dressing.
It's not time to rub the chicken breast.

I like the smell of curry too
But don't be in a hurry
Dinner will soon be served
It's all-you-can-eat don't worry.

I know you want to dive in early
I know she's hot and spicy
Wait! Allow the ingredients of your life and personality
To blend together nicely

Let it marinate; don't manipulate
You can finish everything on your plate
On your wedding date.
I know your knife is sharp
But wait.

Don't penetrate this holy flesh.
It's not time to eat yet.

Conclusion - still on this journey

As I said before...

Sex is a gift; I'll open it after marriage
If I open it now – I know I'll feel like garbage.
I'm waiting till me and my wife are in holy unity
Then I can lose my virginity without feeling guilty.

I've had opportunities to pop a couple cherries
I've had opportunities to get down and dirty
"Go on then!"
But I'm waiting till marriage
I've got water to drink - I'm not thirsty.

It's not easy - I know
Temptation is everywhere making us dizzy.
I just smile it off –
I look at them with a smile that's cheesy.

Trusting God every single day
Relying on Him to lead the way.
Lead me not into temptation
In Jesus' Name, I pray.

The holy life is easy to say
But it's not easy to do.
I'm human – just like you.
I'm tempted – just like you.
I like girls – just like you.
I'm a guy – I have one too.
Everything works down there – that's the truth.

I lean on God's Grace
It's all by His Grace
If not for His Grace

I would be the first one sleeping all over the place.
Then hiding my face.
What a disgrace!
Aren't you the guy who told us to stay in this holy race?

It's been 28 years
I'm still on this purity journey.
Chasing God - not that money
Chasing God - not that honey.
At the right time; all these things will come to me
Just like it says in Matthew 6:33.

I'm human, Lord help me,
Help me to stay on this purity journey.
I'm human, Lord help me,
Help me to stay on this purity journey.
I'm human, Lord help me,
Help me to stay on this purity journey.

I look forward to the day when I will stand and share my
testimony.